SO YOU THINK YOU WANT TO BE A BUDDHIST
2022 EDITION

Norman W. Wilson PhD

SO YOU THINK YOU WANT TO BE A BUDDHIST
2022 EDITION

ZADKIEL PUBLISHING

A ZADKIEL PUBLISHING PAPERBACK

© Copyright 2018
Norman W. Wilson PhD

The right of Norman W. Wilson to be identified as author and channel of this work has been asserted by him in accordance with the Copyright, Designs and Patents Act 1988.

All Rights Reserved

No reproduction, copy or transmission of the publication may be made without written permission.

No paragraph of this publication may be reproduced, copied or transmitted save with the written permission of the publisher, or in accordance with the provisions of the Copyright Act 1956 (as amended).

Any person who does any unauthorised act in relation to this publication may be liable to criminal prosecution and civil claims for damages.

ISBN: 978-1-78695-798-6

Zadkiel Publishing
Is an Imprint of Fiction4All
www.fiction4all.com
This Edition Published 2022

Cover Design by Stephen R Walker Designs
www.srwalkerdesigns.com

INTERIOR FLOWER PHOTOGRAPHY
Suzanne V. Wilson

SECTION PHOTOGRAPHY BY
Aaron Logan, Beria L. Rodriquez, Martin Vorel

COVER PHOTOGRAPHY
Suzanne V. Wilson

DEDICATION

To all who are curious.
Remember, every human being is the author
of his or her own life,
the creator of his or her path.

AUTHOR'S NOTE

I am not a Buddhist nor do I propose I know all there is about this ancient and fascinating belief system. It's doubtful if anyone does. My purpose is a simple one: Provide basic information. I do this as a means of stimulating a reader to investigate and explore further the fundamentals presented here. The more we know about other cultures, the less bigotry, malaise, hatred, and vitriol will flourish

Wherever you go, there you are! A simple statement yet so true! Many upon hearing this statement for the first time almost involuntarily laugh. And yet, here you are, thumbing through these pages. Perhaps it is just idle curiosity, or maybe some long-forgotten desire to learn a little more about Buddhism that has brought you to this little book. Maybe you are seeking answers to questions—questions you may not be aware you have.

One of the standards, traditional, or larger questions you may have is: "Am I on the right path?" The intent of this book is not to answer that question for you, but to help you decide if the Buddhist path is the one for you. You and you alone are the one who chooses, the one who decides.

Norman W. Wilson, Ph.D.
2022

ACKNOWLEDGEMENTS

First and foremost, I am very grateful to Suzanne for her patience, encouragement, and help in bringing this endeavor to life. I am especially appreciative of her wonderful talent as a photographer and for allowing me to use her beautiful flower portraits to illustrate this book. Division photographs are identified and are common usage stock.

Second, I owe a great deal of gratitude to my cover designer, Stephen R Walker. His understanding and perception of the fundamental elements of design are remarkable.

Third, a heartfelt thanks to my publisher, Stuart Holland.

Photo by Aaron Logan. Lightmatter His-Lai Temple. Wikimedia.

CHAPTER ONE

INTRODUCTION AND HISTORICAL OVERVIEW

Have you ever thought about what it would be like to give up your home, your family, friends, and all of your material wealth? What kind of person would leave his wife and family? What could motivate someone to do such a thing? In today's society, deadbeat fathers are not uncommon and their motivations are as varied as they are. However, there is one who left all behind because he believed there was a higher morality and who because of that higher morality, entered upon a most singular quest: *To find a way to rid humankind of its suffering.* His name was not Abraham, Moses, Jesus, or Columbus, or Magellan. Nor was it Pasteur, Salk, or Pauling. Nor was it Mahatma Gandhi or Lhamo Dondrub. Who was this individual? His name was Shakyamuni (Siddhartha) Gautama and he would be called The Buddha. The word, Buddha is Sanskrit and means 'the awakened one.

Scholars have questioned the historical existence of such luminaries as Moses, Zoraster, and Jesus. And like those, scholars also have questioned if there was a historical person called The Buddha. And with time and the advent of modern archaeology evidence has indicated the historical existence of each of these important world-changing figures.

Siddhartha Gautama was born to King Suddhodhana and Queen Maya, rulers of the Sakyas, a tribe of the Gautamas in northern India (today's Nepal) in Lumbini Park at some point during the Sixth Century, BCE. The exact date is not known. It is known that his mother died shortly after his birth and his maternal aunt, Prajapati Gautami, raised him. At age twelve, as was the custom of the day for young Hindu boys, Prince Siddhartha took the Vow of Allegiance to the religion of his fathers. After which he was sent away to the learned priests to learn the *Vedas*. At the end of four years, he returned home to his father's palace whereupon, the sixteen-year-old prince was married to his beautiful young cousin, Princess Yosodhara.

For several years the couple lived within the confines of the royal palace in wondrous luxury, sheltered from all that might be unpleasant. It was not long after their only child was born, a son named Rāhula, that Siddhartha, now twenty-nine went through a series of events that would forever and profoundly change his life and would lead to the *Night of the Great Renunciation.*

Briefly, these events, four in all, dealt with what the young Prince saw as the human condition of his day, and unfortunately would still find to be true in today's world. The first event involved a man writhing in pain, the second involved a crippled old man, the third was a funeral procession, and the fourth involved a beggar monk. No one provided the young Prince with satisfactory answers to his question, why the suffering? After experiencing each of these, the young prince determined to leave his wife and infant son and meditate upon the human condition of pain, old age, and death. With the renunciation of the life of luxury and material substance, Siddhartha began his journey —a journey that would change the world!

We would be remiss not to include here some information about the famous Bo Tree revelations. After seven long years of wandering from place to place, monk after monk, priest after priest, wise man after wise man, Siddhartha gave up the idea of self-immolation and extreme asceticism and accepted the fact that they do not lead to wisdom and they most certainly did not lead to a lessening of mankind's suffering.

It was while resting under a wild fig tree on the bank of the Neranjarā near Gaya in what is now called Bihar, that he formulated what has come to be called "The First Law of Life"– *From good must come good, and from evil must come evil.* After seven days of meditation under this fig tree that is now called the Bo Tree (Tree of Wisdom), Siddhartha went to Isipatana (modern Sarnath) near Benares. There at Deer Park before several of his former colleagues, he delivered his first sermon. It is said that the following episode occurred after this dynamic sermon:

"Are you a god?" asked a young monk.

"No," answered Siddhartha.

"Then, are you a saint?"

"No," came the reply

"If you aren't a god and not a saint, then what are you?"

"I am awake," replied Siddhartha.

From then on, Siddhartha Gautama was called *Buddha*, The Awakened, or The Enlightened. We have included this episode here as a disclaimer to any notion that Siddhartha viewed himself as divinity or viewed himself to be the Son of God.

For nearly a half-century, Buddha went about teaching his philosophy to all that would listen. And at this point, we cannot resist pointing out a fact that is not always emphasized about the Buddha—that he taught all persons regardless of their station in life and regardless of their gender.

Another example from the historical Buddha illustrates an additional important aspect of Buddhism, one with which this book has as its focus.

The story has it that three well-known ascetics, fire-worshippers, listened to the Buddha. One of these, Uruvilva Kasyapa became a follower. Siddhartha and his entourage went to the city of Rajagriha, the capital of Magadha. He had promised King Bimbisara that he would return if he attained bodhi and receive him as his disciple. The King, upon learning of Siddhartha's arrival, went with his counselors and various generals to the place of encampment. There they saw the ascetic Uruvilva Kasyapa with Siddhartha and wondered if he had joined the Enlightened. Uruvilva prostrated himself at the feet of the Buddha thus answering their concerns. On hearing the Buddha, after this incident, King Bimbisara and many of his people became lay followers. And this is the point. One may adopt the Buddhist path without becoming a monk or nun just as one may become a Catholic without becoming a priest or a nun.

By the time the Buddha died at the age of eighty at Kusinārā (located in modern Uttar Pradesh), Buddhism had become an effective moral force in India, a moral force that has lasted nearly three thousand years. With a resurgence of Hinduism in India, Buddhism quickly spread to other countries: Ceylon, Burma, Thailand, China, Korea, Tibet, and Japan. Today it enjoys nearly 535 million members worldwide. In the United States, there are several Buddhist Centers with a total membership of 317,000.

Wherever you go, there you are! [1] A simple statement, yet so true that many people hearing it for the first time almost involuntarily laugh out loud. And yet, here you are, thumbing through these pages. Perhaps it is just an idle curiosity that you have or perhaps it is some long-forgotten desire to learn a little more about Buddhism. And just maybe, lurking in the oasis of your memory there is a hint as to the real reason you are where you are doing what you are doing. So you think you want to be a Buddhist? And you are being bombarded by many unanswered questions, some clearly defined and others vague and unspecified. Some of what you have read is perhaps too complicated, too vague, or too esoteric for your tastes. What follows is an attempt to answer some of those questions and provide you with some basic information about Buddhism.

A Buddhist follows the teachings of Buddha. A Buddhist may be male or female; rich or poor, powerful or powerless, yellow, black, brown or white-skinned. There are no social or status distinctions made in the teachings of Buddha. There are monks, nuns, and lay persons. All accept the fundamental principles taught by the Buddha. As accepting as this sounds, there are still differences among the various schools of Buddhism, however, these differences are more on emphasis and localization than on the actual teachings of the Buddha. And for our purposes here, a summary of these schools is all that is necessary.

The oldest school that is still thriving today is called *Theravada*, literally the "teachings of the elders" and is considered to be the closest to the original teachings of the historical Buddha. Tradition claims that after the death of the Buddha (480 B.C.E.), the first Buddhist Council was called and at this meeting, the sermons delivered by the Buddha and memorized by the bhikkhus (monks) were written down as suttas (Sanskrit: sutra). These sutras or discourses were eventually arranged according to length and subject coming together in three different sets of books called the Tripitaka. The Theravada, also known as the Pali-school [2] or *Hinayana* (hina=lesser; yana=vehicle). Sometimes referred to as "The Lesser Vehicle," the Hinayana school is the most conservative and focuses on the attainment of Enlightenment by the experienced practitioner. Its emphasis is the monastic life and the adherence to those precepts necessary for that life and that means leaving the civilian life with all its attendant material worldliness. Its objective is to bring about an understanding of the impermanence of all things, especially the human body and all its components, to slowly remove the many attachments to the body, attachments to things of this world, and attachments to thoughts, ideas, and desires.

The next school of Buddhism is called *Mahayana* (maha=great; yana=vehicle). Vehicle, as it is used here, means the teachings of the Buddha as the "vehicle" or path to end all suffering. Mahayana, perhaps the larger movement in Buddhism, claims to be for everyone. Enlightenment is still very much its goal, however, it adds a greater focus on Compassion and the Way of the Bodhisattva. It consists of practices that anyone may follow in either the monastic or lay life. This is a sharp difference from the Hinayana approach, which tends to emphasize the ideal of one's end of suffering or cycle of re-birth, one's salvation.

In Mahayana, anyone who is seriously aspiring to be a follower of the Buddha and his teachings makes the Bodhisattva vow. In essence, this vow is a promise to all sentient beings to attain the highest understanding possible, not only for your own sake but also for the sake of all that lives. And with this, it is understood that the final entry into nirvana will be delayed until all sentient beings have received the Dharma (the teaching of the Buddha), thus literally ending ALL suffering in all the known worlds.

Originally flourishing in northern India, the Mahayana school of Buddhism spread over all of Southeast Asia and China. In China, Buddhism was met by a people not unfamiliar with a philosophy very similar to that espoused by the Buddha. Taoism presented a picture of the universe that happened to be in accord with the one presented by the Buddha. Ch'an Buddhism developed during the 6th and 7th centuries and it integrated the idea of the Middle Way, the path between the opposites. Ch'an flourished until the 20th century and the advent of Communism in mainland China.

From China, Ch'an spread to Japan, and there it was met with a minimalist attitude and a disciplined mind which created Zen Buddhism. The focus of Zen Buddhism is the direct experience of Enlightenment. In Zen, the effort is to bring the mind of the practitioner to the same state as that of the Buddha at his moment of Satori. The study of the sutras is important in Zen as it is in the other schools of Buddhism, but for the Zen Buddhist, the greatest importance for the practitioner is Zazen (from which the school's name is derived). Zazen means *sitting*. This involves a highly focused and very simplistic approach to meditation that provides ways of letting all your thoughts come to rest, letting go of the thoughts, until your mind is silent of its noises. Again this is a contrast to the Hinayana School of Buddhism. The emphasis is not on the intellectual study of the Buddha's teachings but rather on the direct Satori experience. Zen

Buddhism became popular in the United States with the advent of the Hippi culture of the late 60s and early 70s. One of its most prolific western writers in the field of Zen is the late Alan Watts.

As is often the case something new and better arises from the ashes of ruin. Buddhism is no exception. With the advent of the Muslim invasions, many of the monasteries were destroyed and the ensuing migration of monks into Tibet and Nepal produced a variation of Mahayana. There in its unique environment, these monks developed the form of Buddhism called *Vajrayana* or The Diamond Vehicle (sometimes called the Lightning Vehicle). It is more mystical than the other Buddhist schools and perhaps because of this, it holds a greater fascination for the Westerner than some of the other forms of Buddhism. Combining with existing ancient tantric practices, this form of Buddhism attempts to integrate all energy aspects of life (anger & sex) as a form of meditation. No event or action that is energy should go wasted–it is all transformed within. Vajrayana attempts to bring you into direct contact with the True Nature of Mind through "magical" practices such as Mantra (chanting), Mudra (hand positions) Tantra (body positions), and Mandala (visualization). You should consider the Vajrayana School only if you have a good foundation in Mahayana teachings because much of the wonderful philosophy that is expressed by these practices wouldn't be understood. Doing a Mantra would have little meaning unless you understood its philosophical significance.

As with all Buddhist schools, the ideal is to dedicate one's life to the teachings of Buddha and the practice of meditation.

In the next few chapters, we will pose questions asked by those that have an interest in Buddhism and provide answers. In this way, we hope that you will begin the necessary foundations for your decision as to what path you should follow, religiously and or spiritually. Namaste!

Photo by Beria L. Rodriquez. Tian Tan Buddha at Hong Kong. June 10, 2013

CHAPTER TWO
SOME BASIC QUESTIONS

Can anyone be a Buddhist or do you have to be a monk or a nun?

Since the focus of this book is on lay Buddhism, its

major emphasis will be in that area. It should be noted that the point of view presented is that of the Therâvada School modified by some aspects of Zen. Further, it should be noted at the outset that there are monks and nuns in

Buddhism who remain celibate and who devote their time to the study of the sutras and follow a monastic life. Anyone may become a Buddhist. As stated earlier, the Buddha recognized no gender or racial distinctions nor did he favor one social class over another. He did not say one had to be a monk or a nun to follow his teachings. You may choose to follow the teachings of the Buddha just as you might choose to follow the teachings of Jesus Christ without becoming a priest or a nun. In truth, you may elect to follow the basic teachings of the Buddha and not be a Buddhist. The reason is simple: the Buddha's teachings are humane and universal.

Does the Buddha expect me to accept his teachings on trust?

One of the things many people find attractive and appealing about Buddhism is that it does not demand that you accept on trust. Such a concept eliminates the debate about whether or not trust is given or earned. The fundamental concept here is that there is freedom from dogma. The Buddha has addressed this issue in his remarks [3]. His statement, "When you know in yourselves" summarizes his position very nicely. The Buddha would have you seek the truth for yourself, whatever it may be. You are free to explore the very nature of ultimate truth. You do not have to do it based on trust in the Buddha. The secret here is that Buddhism does not set up a dogma for you to believe in as do some of the world's major religions; rather it provides things for you to do to arrive at a personal sense of spirituality; practices that have everyday application. Admittedly, for some, such freedom is too much!

Do Buddhist recognize the concept of a creator God?

As far as my research goes, I cannot find any specific reference to a belief in a divine being who created the universe, the earth, and all that it contains. It is indicated in the literature that the Buddha recognized that any answer he would give to this question would cause controversy. The literature does indicate a belief that the universe is subject to the never-ending cycle of birth, death, and rebirth. As a consequence, an absolute beginning is inconceivable.

Is there a "hell" in Buddhism?

There are levels of "hell" in Buddhism but not the ever-lasting eternal condemnation as found in Christianity, for example. Buddhist literature implicitly states there are thirty-one states of existence in our universe. Below the human state exist four levels or planes which are areas of unhappiness. Naraka is probably the closest to the general popular notion of hell. It is a dark and depressing place—a place where there are torments to be experienced by people based on the results of their Kamma. People are born into these levels as a direct result of their unwholesome Kamma—greed, and attachment to worldly goods. Eternal condemnation does not exist in Buddhism. In Buddhism every being is destined for nirvana, even the vilest of individuals are not eternally condemned. You should not interpret this to mean that you are free to do anything you wish. There is a high moral standard of behavior in Buddhism.

What is Kamma?

Karma or Karma is a natural law operating by one's actions. There is no intervention of an outside agent, that is a Devil, for example. For those of you who have a science bent, Kamma is the law of cause and effect, that is for every cause there is an effect.

The same is true in morality. According to the Buddha, Kamma is volition, that is, using one's will. One chooses the action he or she takes and as such he or she is responsible for those actions. Do no harm; do right is sage advice.

There are three misconceptions about kamma. First is the belief that everything that happens is a result of acts done in previous lives; second the belief that all that happens is the result of creation by a Supreme Being, and third, the belief that everything arises without reason or cause.

Are Nibbana and Heaven the same?

First of all, Nibbana (Nirvana) is not a realm, a place of existence as Heaven is depicted in some world religions. If Nibbana is not the same as Heaven, what is it? In an article titled "Nibbana", Thanissaro Bhikkhu states *"We all know what happens when a fire goes out. The flames die down and the fire is gone for good* [4]. Not so. Bhikkhu points out that the fire becomes dormant. Remember, the Second Law of Thermodynamics states energy cannot be destroyed. It can only be transformed. The essence of the flame remains. Narada Thera in "Buddhism In A Nutshell" [5] states, "From a metaphysical standpoint Nibbana is deliverance from suffering. From a psychological standpoint, Nibbana is the eradication of egoism. From an ethical viewpoint, Nibbana is the destruction of lust, hatred, and ignorance." Finally, Nibbana is freedom.

According to Buddhism, can humans be reborn as animals or plants?

Buddhists accept the idea that animals are sentient beings as human beings are sentient. Both contain mind-matter. Animals are subject to the same kammic laws as human beings. One may be reborn in the animal plane because of the degree of Kamma involved. Buddhism does not recognize plants as having the same consciousness as sentient beings. [However, this view may have to change in light of recent scientific breakthroughs in plant studies which suggest communication between plants of the same species, etc.]

Which Buddhist tradition is more popular in the United States and Why?

Buddhism was brought to the United States by immigrants from Asia in the 19th Century and specifically from China right around 1820 and boomed following the Gold Rush in California in 1849. (Pictured is His Lai Temple. Photo by Aaron Logan [6] Today, Buddhism is one of the largest religions in the United States. One of the major reasons for its expansion to non-Asians was the fact that Buddhists do not require any formal 'conversion'. Because one can easily bring dharma practice into his or her daily life it brought in people from every walk of life regardless of their ethnicity, nationality, and or previous religious traditions.

Historically it was the Zen tradition that first entered the United States having been introduced in

California by such famous masters as Shunryu Suzuki and Yasutani Roshi. Zen centers sprouted up in California and eventually spread to the east coast and are now located throughout the United States. The Zen tradition was the first school of Buddhism that entered the mainstream of the American consciousness and became the most popular simply by virtue of its proliferation.

With the ever-growing Tibetan refugees fleeing Chinese Communist domination and with their great desire to preserve the Vajrayana traditions of Tibet the number of Tibetan Lamas who taught this unique form of Buddhism also increased. Because of its seemingly esoteric and exotic nature, Tibetan Buddhism attracted many westerners. Therefore, it too has now spread throughout the North American Continent and winged its way to Europe. With the interest in Buddhism sparked by Zen, the Hinayana tradition with its more conservative approach a stronghold in the United States was firmly established. Because of the wide variety of traditions now available, it should not be a problem for you to locate a place of Buddhist teaching or a local gathering of like-minded people in any of the metropolitan areas. If, however, you live in a rural area such a connection might be more difficult. In that case, your local libraries, bookstores, and the Internet will provide valuable resources for your interests. Most libraries offer inter-library loan options, bookstores will order books for you, and the Internet will offer other valuable sources of information. For your convenience, we have provided a list of books, sites, and sources at the end of this book.

Can anyone visit a Buddhist Temple?

Usually, Buddhist temples are open at all times to anyone who wishes to pay reverence to the Buddha, a Boddhisattva, or the Shangha. However, there may be variations on when the temples are open. You should be aware that the actual ritual approach may vary between the traditions. If you do not know, simply observe others who entered before you. Any monk or another Buddhist will gladly help you and show you the appropriate way.

In all the traditions it is appropriate for you to be casually dressed as you would for any everyday social activity. Swimsuits, cut-offs, bare-midriffs, and shorts are considered inappropriate. Remember you are entering a place of reverence, not a place where you are to show off your body. It is always customary to remove your shoes before entering the temple proper. Most temples have a set of shelves or some other spot where you may leave your shoes. Entering barefoot or in stocking feet is acceptable. Once inside the temple, remain silent. Enter with a slow measured gait. Depending upon the tradition, your hands should be held together, palm to palm, not pressed flat together like a board, but naturally held with no pressure applied to leave some space between your palms. This hand gesture symbolizes the lotus bud. A slight bow from the hip (In Japanese this is called *gassho*) is a sign of respect as you approach the statue of the Buddha. Once in front of the statue, you may light an incense stick, gassho, or some other form of prostration as required by the tradition and or country. Some temples allow simple offerings of fruit, flowers, and occasionally money in front of the statue of the Buddha. In Therâvada tradition the Bhikku (monk) is not allowed to handle money. Finally, it is always in good taste to ask if you are uncertain as to what protocol is expected.

How many years must I go to college to be a Buddhist?

Attendance at a college or university is not a requirement to be a follower of Buddha. To be a Buddhist doesn't just mean to know and understand the teachings of the Buddha, but to *live* them. For learning the path is the best college is life itself. If a Buddhist is not readily available begin by reading the various introductory books on the subject. As your knowledge and understanding increase add more detailed books to your reading list. By all means, make an effort to visit a temple or center where teachers are available. Keep an open mind for not all things are what they seem.

How may I become a Buddhist?

Live and follow the *Eightfold Path* as taught in the Fourth of the Noble Truths of Buddhism. That's all it takes. Generally, this is a journey you must go alone because it involves you; no one else can become a Buddhist for you. Your journey will be made easier if you find fellow human beings that share your aspirations. There is strength in numbers. Visit the local Buddhist temple or center. Though the traditions vary there will be some sort of a formal ceremony to confirm your commitment to be a Buddhist. Yet, you will rarely be required to undergo such a ceremony. Bear in mind, however, that such a ritual can be a very powerful personal experience and can be most helpful in bonding with a local Sangha, a Buddhist community.

One of the simple confirmations of your commitment to being a Buddhist is paying homage to what is called *The Three Jewels.* Just repeat each of the following three statements.

I pay homage to the Buddha.
I pay homage to the Dharma.
I pay homage to the Sangha.

The first of these Three Jewels is the historical Buddha and all the Buddhas of the past and those yet to come. The Second Jewel, the Dharma, the great "thing", is the teachings of the Buddha, the Four Noble Truths including the Eight-fold Path. The Sangha is the community of monks following the path and in the widest sense, everyone within your community and the entire world who has taken it upon themselves to follow the Buddha's teaching, lay Buddhists included. [A lay Buddhist is anyone who follows the Eight Fold Path and is not a Buddhist monk.]

Repeat the homage to the Jewels every day, perhaps in front of a small altar or shrine, you have set up at home. Over time this will help strengthen your commitment and help you overcome the everyday obstacles of life.

What is this going to cost me, and do I have to pay the Buddhist Master?

Before answering this question, please ask yourself: "What is the value of the physical and mental well-being of my Soul?" Can you put a price on your head? In your future? On the future of any sentient being? If you are truly serious about becoming a Buddhist, the greatest sacrifice you will have to make is not money! The price tag is commitment. It will mean making sacrifices to find the time for regular mediation. This means rearranging your schedule of activities, and the time with your family and friends. Hobbies and other interests may have to take a back seat if you are to finalize a quiet time for your meditation. We cannot emphasize this enough: You must make the personal commitment to do your meditation.

With this said—as it is with any religious institution, there is a dependency upon its followers for support. Historically all Buddhist traditions have relied upon the generosity of their lay followers for food, clothing, basic needs, and money. In some countries, Sri Lanka for example, the Buddhist monk leaves the monastery daily to beg for food. However, in our western culture, such an activity would be frowned upon. As with the other major religions that have followers in the West, funds for operating come from the membership. Christian churches take up offerings.

When you visit a Buddhist temple or center or when you engage a Buddhist teacher it is appropriate to make a monetary contribution. It is also necessary for us to remind you that to truly live, as Zen teaches, is free; money is not required.

Is it true that Buddhist Masters beat their students with long poles to make them pay attention?

Ah, the fear of pain! As soon as people hear about the infamous Encouragement Stick their minds are filled with grotesque images of bygone days when teachers beat their students with rulers or fathers beat their sons with switches cut from Sycamore Trees. Unfortunately, during the early days of Zen in America, the use of the Encouragement Stick was indeed abused. Horror stories of bloody backs and shoulders of students returning from a meditation session abound. Fear not! The *kyosaku* of the Soto or the *kaisaku* of the Rinzai schools, as these sticks are called, are seldom used outside of Japan.

To allay any concerns, you might have about the use of these sticks in any Buddhist center you are considering simply ask at that center. In addition, in the rare event they are used, you may request that the stick is not used on you. Never hesitate or be embarrassed to ask about any rituals, ceremonies, or customs at any center.

There is a justification for the use of the Encouragement Stick and we want to explain that to you at this point. First, the use of the stick is based upon the Mahayana concept of *upaya* or "skillful means". For the stick to have a positive and useful result, it must be applied skillfully and at the right moment. Finding the right moment does indeed require skillful observation by the Zen Master or senior monk. Walking around beating on students' shoulders randomly serves no purpose other than to cause pain. In traditional Zen monasteries, the Master or monk quietly walked behind the meditating students and if a student was found lacking in posture or if his mind was wandering he would receive a light tap on his shoulder to hint that a blow was about to be struck. The student would then bow slightly and a well-placed sharp blow was applied. After the blow, both the student and the monk would bow in the traditional gesture of gratitude (gassho). The sudden impact of the stick is said to clear the mind, return the student to his former level of concentration, and in some cases even bring the concentration to higher levels. It is not unheard of that students to request the application of the stick and in some instances, a student by the mere sound of the stick gained sudden insight or enlightenment! The purpose of the Encouragement Stick was to help maintain concentration and was never intended as an instrument of brutality.

Is Buddha God?

When one asks if is Buddha God what is being asked if he is the Creator of the Universe, of the earth, of man, and all other living and non-living entities? The Buddha never referred to himself as a Divinity. The acceptance of the notion of an omnipotent creator deity or a prime mover (remember that from philosophy?) is a key distinction between the other major world religions and Buddhism. When asked if he was God, Buddha replied with a very simple "No!" When asked what he was Buddha replied, "I am awake!"

Buddhists neither deny nor accept the idea of a creator; nor do they endorse any views about creation. Buddhist maintain any question about the origin of the world is worthless. For the practitioner, any dogmatic belief in a Supreme Being is a hindrance to the attainment of Nirvana. A word of caution here—despite this apparent disdain and non-theism, the Buddhists believe the veneration of the Noble Ones to be very important.

Further, Buddhists do accept the existence of beings in the higher realms, called *devas*. Deva is one of many different types of non-human beings who share godlike characteristics of being more powerful, longer-lived, and, in general, much happier than humans. Devas do not receive the same level of veneration paid to them as is paid to buddhas. It is important to note these existent beings in the higher realms are not necessarily wiser than the rest of the human beings.

What is the purpose or aim of Buddhism?

Perhaps to some readers, the answer to this question may seem selfish.

It is not! The sole aim of spiritual practice for the Buddhists is the complete alleviation of stress from samsara—the life cycle of birth, death, and rebirth.

What is the Buddhist position on violence?

Because Buddhist practice nonviolence does not mean he or she is submissive, a wimp, or a coward. The basic cause of violence is the entanglement of extreme ideas. Generally, this happens when one becomes entangled in the issues of good/bad, moral/immoral, or ugly/beautiful. This dualism often takes on the posture of inflexible self-righteousness. Certainly, a person who is a Buddhist will defend her or himself.

If I become a Buddhist, do I have to go out and proselytize?

Unlike some of the other world religions, in Buddhism, there is no expectation that you should go out and attempt to convert others to Buddhism. A practicing Buddhist never advocates bloodshed in the name of Buddhism as a conversion mechanism.

Does a Buddhist pursue happiness as a life goal?

Unfortunately, and all too often, people list happiness as a goal to be achieved, much as they would have as a goal of buying a house or an automobile. Many individuals maintain the only happiness that can be achieved comes after an earthly death and a rebirth into heaven. For the followers of Buddhism, heaven is not a place; it's a release from the notion of dualism. The goal for Buddhists is to be free from dualism, confusion, and suffering. For the Buddhists, Nirvana is neither happiness nor unhappiness. It simply is.

As a Buddhist, do I have to give up sex?

Absolutely not! If you become a Buddhist monk, nun, or priest you must practice celibacy. However, in Japan, a monk or a nun may marry. Generally speaking, these practitioners are not viewed as monks or nuns by "old school" Buddhists. You do not have to be a monk, nun, or priest to follow the Buddhist path any more than you have to be a Catholic to follow a Christian path.

Buddhist Temple-Thai. Photo by Papos. August 24, 2011. Pixabay.

CHAPTER THREE
Statistically Speaking

Buddhism is among the world's most important religions. When compared to Christianity, Islam, or Hinduism, Buddhism ranks fourth with 535 million members. [7] Do not equate its rank as a reference to Buddhism's importance in the world order of things. There are three main branches of Buddhism: Theravada (150 million adherents located in Cambodia, Thailand, Laos, Sri Lanka, and Myanmar), Mahayana (360 million members spread throughout China, South Korea, Taiwan, Singapore, Vietnam, and Japan.), and Vajrayana frequently called Tibetan Buddhism (approximately 18 million adherents living in Tibet Autonomous Region, Bhutan, Mongolia, and India).

Buddhist American scholar, Charles Prebish indicates there are three broad types of American Buddhism. The oldest, ethnic Buddhism, arrived in America already adherents. The second group and perhaps the one that is the most visible came here in response to the interest shown by American converts. The third group, the Evangelical Buddhists are located in another country but actively recruits members in the United States.

The initial problem in accurately determining the number of Buddhist adherents is the lack of a central office for counting the numbers. Further, many practice Buddhist meditations but do not consider themselves adherents. The best current estimate of the number of Buddhists in the United States is roughly two to three million.

The city of Tallmadge, California has the largest Buddhist community in the western hemisphere. It is called The City of Ten Thousand Buddhas and is housed on 480 acres.

**Photo by Aaron Logan. Lightmatter His-Lai
Temple Garden,
San Gabriel, Valley, California.**

CHAPTER FOUR
On Being A Buddhist Monk or Nun

Being a Buddhist monk or nun means living your  life following the Vinaya, the monastic rules. These rules very clearly state, and do so right up front, that if you engage in sexual intercourse you are not a monk or nun anymore. There is an automatic exclusion from ordination.

There are no exceptions to the requirements of abstinence. There are no Tibetan monks or nuns who marry. Nuns, because they wear almost identical clothing as do the monks, are often mistaken for monks. Perhaps an easy way to distinguish between a nun and a monk is by their hair. Monks always have shaved heads. The bhikkhuni may have long uncut hair which is piled on top of the back of their heads.

The situation in Japan is different where the Vinaya was abolished several centuries ago. Generally and technically, those who are identified as monks and or nuns, are not in the Tibetan sense. That includes those who have their heads shaved and live a celibate life in a monastery. Because they do not follow the Vinaya, those individuals are considered priests and as such, they may marry.

The prohibition of sexual intercourse for monks is such an important rule of traditional Buddhism that it is the very first rule of the Vinaya and there are over 200 such rules.

Bell at Lightmatter His-Lai Temple. Photo by Aaron Logan

CHAPTER FIVE
The Question of An Omnipotent Creator and Devas

A key distinction between Buddhism and other

major world religions revolves around the question of adhering to the idea of an omnipotent creator deity. Some refer to this as *the prime mover*, the initial agent that is the
cause of all things. For the Buddhists, there is a belief in non-adherence to the idea of a divinity that created the world and all that is in it.

To believe in a supreme god would, for the Buddhist, create an obstacle to the attainment of Nirvana—the highest goal of the Buddhist belief system. However, just because there is a non-adherence to the dogmatic belief in a supreme being does not mean Buddhists do not consider veneration of the Noble Ones as being important. "The word "noble," or ariya, is used by the Buddha to designate a particular type of person, the type of person which it is the aim of his teaching to create. In the discourses, the Buddha classifies human beings into two broad categories. On one side there are the puthujjanas, the worldlings, those belonging to the multitude, whose eyes are still covered with the dust of defilements and delusion. On the other side, there are the ariyans, the noble ones, the spiritual elite, who obtain this status not from birth, social station or ecclesiastical authority but their inward nobility of character."[8]

Admittedly, there is a minor difference between the two main Buddhist traditions. The Theravada Buddhists view the Buddha as a human being that attained Nirvana or Buddhahood through his humanitarian efforts. However, the Mahayana Buddhists consider The Buddha as the embodiment of the cosmos, who was born for the benefit of others and was not just a human being.

Buddhists do accept the existence of beings in the higher realms. these being are called *devas* and like humans, they suffer. Furthermore, they are not necessarily wiser than normal human beings. Devas do live longer than humans and are considered more powerful than humans. They are invisible to the human eye much like spirits in other belief systems. Under certain circumstances or conditions, a human being may experience a deva visually or by auditory perception. When such an event occurs to you, welcome the deva.

The devas are divided into three classes depending upon which of the three realms into which they were born. There are devas with no physical form or location, and they do not interact with the rest of the cosmos. The second group does have a physical form, is sexless, and lacks any form of passion. This group has five subgroups. The third group of devas have a physical form much like humans but are larger. They live very much like humans. They live longer than humans.

Photo by Aaron Logan Lightmatter His-Lai-Temple.

CHAPTER SIX
The Difference Between Devas and Gods

Unfortunately, the English translation of the word *deva* equates it to God or angel. Devas are neither Gods nor angels. First, devas do not create. They did not create the universe, the earth, or its inhabitants—human, animal, or plant. Devas come into being, existence based on their past and are subject to the natural law of cause and effect just as are all other living and nonliving things of this world.

Furthermore, devas are not immortal. Even though they live for a very long time, their lifespan is not finite. When they die, they are reborn as some other entity. This new entity might be a human being, a different type of deva, or something alien to our human understanding.

Devas are not incarnations of archetypal deities or manifestations as discussed by the late Swiss psychiatrist and psychoanalyst. Carl Jung. Like human beings, devas are considered to be distinct individuals with distinct personalities who follow their life paths. Do not confuse devas as mere symbols. They are not. Within their being, devas have a potential Buddha nature just as humans do.

Unlike deities in other religions, devas are not omniscient or omnipotent. Nor are they morally perfect. Depending upon the class, some devas may be ignorant, arrogant, and prideful. Some may even exhibit lust, jealousy, or anger. Furthermore, Buddhists do not give specific importance to such deities. Nor do they view these deities as the foundational support for the oral development of their adherents. Buddhists do not render credit to these deities for the attainment of salvation.

Despite the belief that both human beings and devas are perishable, a common belief among many Buddhists is that these deities can be influenced to grant their favors. This is accomplished by the human being transferring merits to the devas whenever meritorious deeds are performed. Making offerings and worshiping these deities are not encouraged.

A thorough search of Buddhist teachings does not reveal that one may attain Nirvana by praying to any deity. Since moral and immoral behavior depends on oneself, the Buddhist believes no one from the outside can purify another.

Photo by Martin Vorel. Buddhist Monastery with Stupa, Thailand. September 9, 2007.

CHAPTER SEVEN
Nirvana And Heaven

Followers of Buddhism accept the fact that the life in which they are now is only a temporary vessel composed of body, emotions, thoughts, and knowledge. Such a belief promotes the notion that in this life, there is no sense of self or soul. This is a significant aspect of the Buddhists' central theme that one is to break the death/birth cycles. Be forewarned, Nirvana is not the same as the Christian or Islamic Heaven.

For the Buddhists, Nirvana is being free from suffering and personal or individual existence. This state or condition is called Enlightenment or transcendental knowledge (Bodhi). Gaining Enlightenment is the goal of all Buddhists. It is significant because it breaks the otherwise endless cycle of reincarnation. The Buddha has called Nirvana "the highest happiness." It is a state free of craving, anger, and other conflicting states.

At this point, considerable care is necessary to avoid misunderstanding. This peace is achieved whenever all the existing and willing formations have been established within the countless incarnations and are pacified, and any inclinations for the production of new ones are removed. This means all underlying dispositions which are the basis for repeated incarnations, no longer exist.

Attaining this state of Nirvana in either the present life or some future life depends on one's effort. Nirvana is not pre-determined.

The concept of heaven(s) is quite commonplace in religious, cosmological, and or transcendent systems. Generally, it is a realm inhabited by gods, angels, spirits, saints, and or ancestors. Heaven is viewed as a higher place, a place where one wants to be. It is frequently described as Paradise and is accessible by human beings who have lived exemplary lives.

In Buddhism, there are many heavens. One suggested the figure is thirty-three heavens. Unlike some of the other major world religions, Buddhists do not accept the notion that these heavens are eternal and there is no physical and permanent place called heaven.

**Photo by Martin Vorel. Emerald Buddha.
Thailand.
September 2, 2004**

CHAPTER EIGHT
The Antithesis of Nirvana

Samsara (sometimes spelled Sansara) means a continuous movement or flow. It refers to the daily activities of the regular world, which includes all the trivialities, anger, jealousies, frustrations, and desires human beings exhibit. For Buddhists, Samsara is the cycle of birth, decay, and death. All beings in the universe participate in this natural phenomenon.

Samsara is continuous suffering: Spiritual, physical, and emotional. The Buddhist term for this continuous suffering is *dukkha*. The notion of evil is not necessarily associated with Samsara. In Buddhism, evil has no essence or substance of its own; it is a human label loosely used to describe a wide variety of actions. In essence, evil is a product of impermanent causes and conditions.

The idea of Samsara is a carryover from the ancient Hindu belief of reincarnation. It is from the Hindus that Siddhartha Gautama, the Buddha, developed some of his teachings about life and death. Such borrowing does not diminish the interpretation and application given by Siddhartha Gautama.

The role of the follower of Buddha is to get rid of those aspects of one's life that cause suffering. One is to seek and strive for enlightenment.

Photo by Martin Vorel. The Golden Buddha, Thailand. 2014

CHAPTER NINE
The Devil

Mara, the Evil One, is the closest concept to the Devil there is in Buddhism. He is among the first non-human beings presented in Buddhist scriptures and represents temptation, sin-of-all unwholesome impulse, and spiritual death. he is often called the Tempter. Sometimes, however, he is called the Lord of Death. Yet, Mara is frequently simply viewed as a nuisance.

There are, in traditional Buddhism, four senses of the word Mara. First, is the sense in which Mara is the embodiment of all unskillful emotions. The second sense is that of death in terms of the ceaseless rounds of birth and death. The third, is a metaphor for what may be called *conditional existence*. The fourth and final sense is viewed as Mara, the son of a deva. In this case, it references an objectively existent being, rather than a metaphor.

In Buddhism, there is a literal and psychological interpretation of Mara as a physical entity and as a psychological metaphor for the various processes of self-doubt and temptation that block and hinder spiritual endeavors.

Mara is significant in the life of Buddha. His story of temptation is a well-known experience in other world religions, also. Mara is an obstacle to the attainment of Buddhahood. Mara tempts Siddhartha three times. First, the world is offered as a place which he could rule. This brought no response from Siddhartha. Second, Mara offered up his most beautiful daughters to seduce Siddhartha. It didn't work because he remained in a state of meditation. Third, an army of monsters was sent to attach the defenseless Siddhartha. He remained seated and untouched. Finally, in desperation, Mara challenged Siddhartha to say who would speak up for him. Siddhartha raised his right hand and touched the earth. The earth spoke up for Siddhartha and Mara disappeared. The Buddha was born!

CHAPTER TEN
Evil and Karma

Evil, like so many other things in Buddhism, has no

substance in itself. It's a name given to impermanent causes and conditions. There is not a permanent perpetrator such as the Devil in Christianity. Remember, the māra is not the exact equivalent of the Devil in Buddhism. There are three causes of evil or three poisons as they are sometimes called. These poisons are ignorance, attachment, and aversion. It is these there that keep sentient beings trapped in samsara. An examination of the Wheel of Life indicates these three poisons lead to the creation of *karma*.

Today, like so many other words, karma is all too often misused. In Buddhism, karma is not fate; nor is it a cosmic justice system that delivers rewards and or punishments.

Simply put, karma is cause and effect. Human beings create karma and they do so with very specific and intentional acts of the body, speech and thought (mind). The only acts that do not produce karma are those which are free of desire, hate, and delusion.

Of the three poisons, ignorance is to be the root; the basis upon which the others are built. From it, attachment and aversion arise. Aversion shows itself in sentient beings as anger, revulsion, hatred, dislike, fear, and indifference.

Ringu Tulka in his book *Daring Steps Toward Fearlessness: The Three Vehicle of Tibetan Buddhism states,* "Ignorance is equivalent to the identification of self as being separate from everything else.

CHAPTER ELEVEN
Wisdom and the Four Noble Truths

Asking what wisdom is, is as complicated as asking what life is. A standard dictionary definition of wisdom states "wisdom is accumulated knowledge with common sense." That really helps. So, what do we mean by *common sense*? Imagine, for a moment, what it might be like listening to the early Greek philosophers as they held forth on what each of these terms meant. Such a discourse could go on for days.

For Buddhists, wisdom has a singularly different connotation. Wisdom embodies the understanding of the Four Noble Truths. And that is a very large order. Intellectual understanding is not sufficient. One must transform this understanding into very real and personal facts. The Buddhist philosophy calls for the cultivation of good conduct and mental development. Simply reading about the Four Nobel Truths is not the same as attaining wisdom. A personal demonstration is necessary and is required.

Buddhist traditions indicate the Four Noble Truths were a part of the first lesson Buddha taught after his Enlightenment, and are pivotal in Buddhist thought. In that discourse, an explanation of *dukkha* (suffering) was given to his first five disciples at Sarnath, India. All the Truths deal with some aspect of suffering.

The First Noble Truth of dukkha is birth, illness, aging, sorrow, pain, grief, despair, and death. There is more to this than the general usage of suffering. It refers to the fundamental unsatisfactory nature of all life forms because they are not permanent. Westerners will equate this as being very pessimistic. In reality, it is simply an attempt to identify the nature of dukkha. It's just being truthful.

The Second Noble Truth of dukkha is craving, lust, seeking delight, craving for sensual pleasures, and existence. Craving is conditioned by ignorance. Ignorance refers to misunderstanding the nature of the Self and reality. Do not consider this to be an abonnement of pleasure. It is not! If that were the case, we would not have Buddhists today. In today's world, we have people who commit themselves to institutional care because of being "obsessed" with sex or because they are alcoholics, porno addicts, drug addicts, and food addicts.

The Third Noble Truth is the cessation of dukkha; that is, the relinquishing of craving. It is the cessation of all unsatisfactory experiences and their causes in such a way that it becomes impossible for them to reoccur. Cessation becomes the goal of one's Buddhist spiritual practice.

The Fourth Noble Truth is the way leading to the cessation of suffering and involves the right view, intention, right action, mindfulness, and right livelihood. Involved here is the Noble Eightfold Path and it is considered to be the very essence of Buddhist practice. The Noble Eightfold Path is composed of the Right Understanding, Right

Thought, Right Speech, Right Action, Right Livelihood, Right Effort, Right Mindfulness, and Right Concentration. Each of these is explained in the next chapter.

Photo by Martin Vorel. Buddhist Monks. Thailand. 2007

CHAPTER TWELVE
The Noble Eightfold Path

The Nobel Eightfold Path is the means through which enlightenment may be realized. Do not construe this to mean eight steps or stages in which each has to be completed before moving on to the next step. View these as highly significant aspects of one's behavior, dependent upon one another, and when taken as a whole, can define a way of living.

Right Understanding is sometimes called Right View or Wisdom Path. Whichever name is used, this path is absolutely not about believing in a doctrine. It is about perceiving the true nature of human beings (actually all sentient beings) and the world in which they exist.

Right Intention also called Right Thought, or Right Attitude, encompasses an emotional intelligence in one's life—a life in which acts are based on love and compassion.

Right Speech supposes clear, thoughtful, and non-harmful communication.

Right Action involves an ethical foundation for life which is based upon the pinion of non-exploitation. Non-exploitation includes oneself as well as others.

Right Livelihood, sometimes called Proper Livelihood, is based upon the fundamental principle of non-exploitation.

Right Effort, Vitality, or Right Diligence is a conscious directing of one's energy forces to the path of creative healing actions that foster wholeness.

Right Mindfulness, sometimes called Though Awareness, necessitates one being aware of all things—one's feelings, thoughts, and that which is most real.

Right Concentration requires the development of a mental discipline to cut through delusion. It's an absorption of the mind on a fixed and single object. meditation is strongly suggested for this achievement.

When combined, The Nobel Eightfold Path is a marvelous blueprint for a high-ended moral system.

**Photo by Martin Vorel. Wooden Temple.
Thailand. January 2007**

LIST OF TEMPLES IN THE UNITED STATES AND GREAT BRITAIN

California

    Abhayagiri Buddhist Monastery
    Berkeley Buddhist Monastery
    Berkeley Zen Center
    City of Ten Thousand Buddhas
    Fresno Buddhist Temple
    Green Gulch Farm Zen Center
    Hartford Street Zen Center
    Hazy Moon Zen Center
    Hsi Lai Temple
    Koyasan Buddhist Temple
    Mount Baldy Zen Center
    Oroville Chinese Temple
    Pao Fa Temple
    San Fran Dhammaram Temple
    San Francisco Zen Center
    Senshin Buddhist Temple
    Shasta Abbey
    Sonoma Mountain Zen Center
    Tassajara Zen Mountain Center
    Thubten Dhargye Ling
    Wat Buddhanusorn
    Wat Mongkolratanaram
    Yokoji Zen Mountain Center
    Zenshuji

Florida

    Guang Ming Temple
    Tubten Kunga Center
    Wat Florida Dhammaram
    Wat Mongkolratanaram (Tampa, Florida

Hawaii

    Broken Ridge Buddhist Temple
    Daifukuji Soto Zen Mission
    Hawaii Shingon Mission

Illinois

    Buddhist Temple of Chicago
    Chicago Zen Center
    Daiyuzenji

Massachusetts

    Cambridge Zen Center
    Valley Zendo
    Wat Boston Buddha Vararam
    Wat Nawamintararachutis

New Mexico

    Bodhi Manda Zen Center
    Hokoji Zendo
    Kagyu Shenpen Kunchab
    Kagyu Shenpen Kunchab Bodhi Stupa
    Upaya Institute and Zen Center

Zuni Mountain Stupa

New York

Bodhi Manda Zen Center
Hokoji Zendo
Kagyu Shenpen Kunchab
Kagyu Shenpen Kunchab Bodhi Stupa
Upaya Institute and Zen Center
Zuni Mountain Stupa

Texas

American Bodhi Center
Chua Buu Mon
Chua Linh-Son Buddhist Temple
Jade Buddha Temple (Houston)
Maria Kannon Zen Center
Wat Buddhananachat of Austin
Wat Buddhavas of Houston

England

Chithurst Forest Monastery
Dhamma Talaka Pagoda
Kadampa Buddhist Temple
Norwich Buddhist Centre
Wat Charoenbhavana

SOME BASIC BUDDHIST QUOTATIONS

The following quotations are offered as points for your contemplation. Enjoy!

Your worst enemy cannot harm you as much as your own unguarded thoughts. (Sutta Nipata)

What is the world condition? Body is the world condition. And with body and form goes feelings, perception, consciousness, and all the activities throughout the world.

The arising of form and the ceasing of form— everything that has been heard, sensed and known, sought after and reached by the mind—all this is the embodied world, to be penetrated and realized. (Samyutta Nkikeya)

*Make an island of yourself,
make yourself your refuge;
there is no other refuge.
Make truth your island,
make truth your refuge;
there is no other refuge. (Digha Nikaya)*

*Do not purse the past.
Do not lose yourself in the future.
The past no longer is.
The future has not yet come. (Bhaddekaratta Sutta)*

BIBLIOGRAPHY

Bachelor, Stephen. Buddhism Without Beliefs: A Contemporary Guide to Awakening. Riverhead Trade. New York. 1998.

Carus, Paul. History of the Devil and the Ideas and Evil from the Earliest Times to the Present Day. Nabu Press. Charleston, S.C. 2010.

Conze, Edward. Buddhist Meditation. Harper Row. New Yor. 1956.

Das, Lama Surya. Buddha Is As Buddha Does. San Francisco Harper. San Francisco, CAL. 2007.

Dalai Lama. How to Practice: The Way to a Meaningful Life. Atria Books. New York. 2003.

Eliade, Mircea, Ioan P. Couliano with Hillary S. Wiesner. The Harper Collins Concise Guide to World Religions. Harper Collins. New York. 2000.

Geshe, Sonam Rinchen. How Karma Works: The Twelve Links of Dependent Arising. Snow Lion. Ithaca, New York. 2006.

Hanh, Tich Nhat. The Heart of Buddha. Harmony Books. New York. 1997.

Keowen, Damien. Dictionary of Buddhism. Oxford University Press. London. 2004.

Khyentse, Dsongsar, Jamyang. What Makes You Not A Buddhist. Shambhala. Boston. 2008.

Mitchell, Donald w. Buddhism: Introducing the Buddhist Experience. Oxford University Press. 2nd Ed. New York. 2007.

Suzuki, Daisetz Teitara, and Christmas Humphreys. An Introduction to Zen Buddhism. Grove Press. New York. 1994.

Suzuki, Daietz Teitara. Zen Buddhism. Three Rivers Press. New York. 1996.

Suzuki, Shunryu. Zen Mind. Beginners' Mind. Shambhala. Boston. 2006

Wright, Robert. Why Buddhism is True. Simon & Schuster. New York. 2017.

FOOTNOTES

[1] Also the title of a book written by Jon Kabat-Zinn. Hyperion. New York, 1994.

[2] Pali is the language the sermons of the Buddha were written in and is a variation of the ancient Indian language called Sanskrit.

[3] Made to the Kalamas, a tribe who lived in the vicinity of Kesaputta.

[4] 1996. From a printed copy included in *Noble Strategy*. San Diego. Metta Forest Monistery. 1999.

[5] 1982. Buddhist Publication Society. Kandy. Sri Lanka

[6] From http://www.lightmatter.net/gallery/albums.pht.CC By 1.0, http://commons.wikimedia.org/w/index.php?curd=13570

[7] According to the figures presented in 2013.

[8] *Ajahn Sucitto (2010), Turning the Wheel of Truth: Commentary on the Buddha's First Teaching, Shambhala*

www.ingramcontent.com/pod-product-compliance
Lightning Source LLC
Chambersburg PA
CBHW061507040426
42450CB00008B/1518

* 9 7 8 1 7 8 6 9 5 7 9 8 6 *